Let's Talk About Pets

SLITHERING SNAKES
and how to care for them

David and Patricia Armentrout

ROURKE PUBLISHING

www.rourkepublishing.com

www.rourkepublishing.com

Photo credits: Cover © fivespots; Contents © fivespots; Page 4 © Eric Isselée; Page 5 © B.Stefanov; Page 6 © Joel Kempson; Page 8 © Audrey Snider-Bell; Page 9 © Eric Isselée; Page 10 © forestpath; Page 11 © fivespots; Page 12 © Eric Isselée; Page 13 © Lucian Coman ; Page 14 © Blue Door Publishing; Page 16/17 © Dhoxax; Page 18/19 © Stephen Kiers; Page 20 © Ryan Kelm; Page 21 © RLHambley; Page 22 © Theodore Garland, Jr.

Editor: Jeanne Sturm

Cover and page design by Nicola Stratford, bdpublishing.com

Library of Congress Cataloging-in-Publication Data

Armentrout, David, 1962-
 Slithering snakes and how to care for them / David and Patricia Armentrout.
    p. cm. -- (Let's talk about pets)
 Includes bibliographical references and index.
 ISBN 978-1-61590-248-4 (Hard cover) (alk. paper)
 ISBN 978-1-61590-488-4 (Soft cover)
 1. Snakes as pets--Juvenile literature. I. Armentrout, Patricia, 1960- II. Title.
 SF459.S5A76 2011
 639.3'96--dc22
                                    2010012386

Rourke Publishing
Printed in the United States of America, North Mankato, Minnesota
033010
033010LP

www.rourkepublishing.com - rourke@rourkepublishing.com
Post Office Box 643328 Vero Beach, Florida 32964

TABLE OF CONTENTS

ball python

WILD ABOUT SNAKES

Are you wild about snakes? When you spot a slithering snake in the garden, are you eager to catch and hold it?

If you are curious about the way snakes live and behave, it may make sense to have one as a pet. Snakes are fascinating **reptiles**, and some **species** make awesome pets.

Reptile Reality

Some people dislike, or even fear, snakes. Make sure everyone in your home shares your interest in getting a pet snake.

corn snake

albino corn snake

Corn snakes often have bold color combinations of orange, red, brown, and black, but no two corn snakes will have the same color pattern.

Before getting a snake, consider its needs and your role as a caregiver.

• Your snake will spend most of its time in an enclosure, needing only about ten minutes of playtime, or handling, each day.

• Snakes are **carnivorous**. Pet snakes eat live or pre-killed whole **prey** animals like mice and rats. It is important that everyone in your home understands and is comfortable with the way your snake feeds.

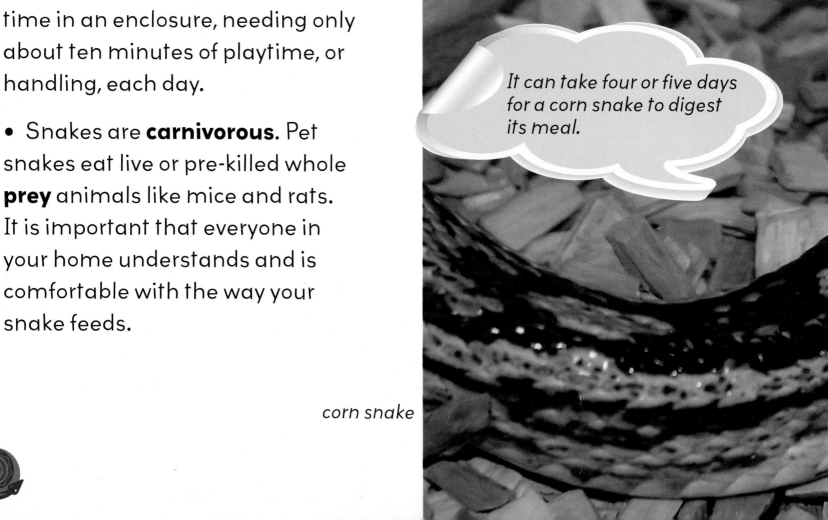

It can take four or five days for a corn snake to digest its meal.

corn snake

6

Pet snakes live, on average, 20 years. Caring for a snake is a long-term time commitment. If for any reason you no longer can care for your snake, you must not release it into the wild. It is illegal, and dangerous for your pet. You will need to find a **breeder** or someone who can give your snake a good home.

CHOOSING THE RIGHT SNAKE

There are nearly 3,000 kinds of snakes, but very few make good pets. In fact, you don't want a **venomous** snake! A venomous snake uses fangs to inject poison into prey before feeding.

Rattlesnakes ARE NOT good pets. Their bite can be DEADLY!

western diamondback rattlesnake

A non-venomous snake like a corn snake or a king snake is a great choice for a new snake owner. Both have beautiful color patterns, are **docile**, and only reach about five feet (1.5 meters) long when fully grown.

Reptile Reality

Get your snake from a breeder. A captive-bred snake is typically healthier and has a calmer personality than a wild snake.

California king snake

Most pet gopher snakes have calm personalities. However, some hiss loudly or even strike with opened mouths when disturbed.

gopher snake

milk snake

Milk snakes are bred in a wide variety of colors and make great pets.

Rosy boas are popular choices for first-time snake owners because they are slow moving, docile, and easy to care for.

rosy boa

11

SNAKE SPECIFICS

Did you know a snake smells with its tongue? It flicks its tongue out to collect particles from the air. Then, it quickly brings the tongue to a special organ inside its mouth to examine the particles. That's how a snake senses, or smells, things in its environment.

rat snake

12

gopher snake

Snakes also have to move in and out of warm and cool places to control their body temperatures. They do this because they are **ectotherms**. They do not make their own heat like people. Your snake enclosure will need a warm side and a cool side so your pet can live comfortably.

Wild snakes bask in the sun for warmth.

HOMEY HABITAT

Your snake will be happy in an enclosure that looks and feels like a natural snake habitat. Setting up the enclosure is easy when you use your supply checklist.

ball python

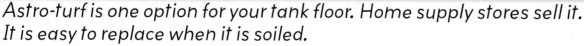

Astro-turf is one option for your tank floor. Home supply stores sell it. It is easy to replace when it is soiled.

Snake Habitat Supply Checklist

☑ An aquarium tank with a tight-fitting screen lid that locks closed. Use a 10-gallon (38-liter) tank for a small, young snake, or a 20-gallon (76-liter) tank for an adult snake.

☑ At least one heat source to create a warm side of the enclosure; either an electric warming mat for the underside of the tank or an aluminum-type clip lamp.

☑ Shredded newspaper for the tank floor.

☑ A plastic box, or other type of object with an opening that your snake can slither into and hide.

☑ A sturdy, shallow water dish for drinking and soaking. Place it at the cool side of the tank.

☑ Thermometers to measure air temperature. The cool side should measure between 70 and 75 degrees Fahrenheit (21 and 24 degrees Celsius), the warm side between 82 and 86 degrees Fahrenheit (28 and 30 degrees Celsius).

☑ A **humidity** gauge to measure moisture level. Tank humidity should measure between 40 and 60 percent.

HOW TO FEED YOUR SNAKE

You can buy live or frozen feeder mice from a breeder or pet store. Keep frozen mice in your home freezer. Your snake should eat one mouse, about the size of the widest part of its body, every 7 to 14 days.

Reptile Reality

In the wild, many non-venomous snakes use **constriction** to kill prey before feeding. They have teeth, but use them to grab, not to chew. Snakes swallow their meals whole.

Burmese python

Feeding your snake pre-killed rats or mice will prevent injuries to your pet caused by struggling prey.

These are not good pets for inexperienced owners.

Before feeding your snake frozen food, thaw it completely. Move your snake to a separate box so it does not think of its enclosure as a hunting ground.

After feeding, put your snake back in its habitat and do not handle it for two days. Snakes need to rest after they eat. Too much handling or movement after feeding can cause them to vomit.

Reptile Reality

Wash your hands before and after feeding and handling your snake. If your snake smells food on your hands, it may mistake your hands for a meal.

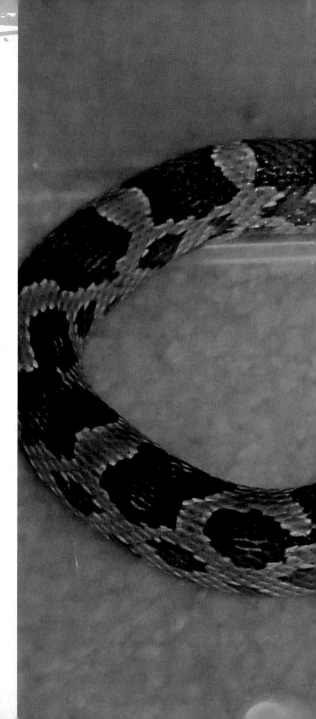

THE SKINNY ON SHEDDING

Did you know that snakes' skin is dry and smooth, not slimy? And, because it doesn't stretch, snakes have to shed layers of skin as they grow. Young snakes grow at a more rapid rate, and will shed more frequently, than older snakes.

You'll know your snake is about to shed if it refuses to eat, its eyes turn cloudy, and its skin color looks dull.

Healthy snakes will typically shed their skin in one piece.

A tree branch or rock from a pet store looks nice in the enclosure, and gives your snake something to climb and rub against when shedding.

ball python

21

DO'S AND DON'TS OF SNAKE CARE

Do clean the enclosure and water dish regularly. A clean home protects your pet from harmful germs. Do take your snake to a **veterinarian** if you notice unusual behaviors, or suspect it is ill. Your snake's health depends on you.

Don't pick up your snake by its head, or wrap your snake around your neck. Instead, grab your snake at the center of its body and support it with two hands. Don't be surprised if it curls around your wrist. Your snake just wants to feel safe and secure.

Have fun observing your snake. You'll find it's easy to give your snake great care when you understand how it lives and behaves.

rosy boa

GLOSSARY

breeder (BREED-ur): someone who mates animals to produce certain characteristics

carnivorous (kar-NIV-ur-uhss): meat-eating

constriction (kuhn-STRIKT-shun): slowing or stopping air flow by squeezing

docile (DOSS-uhl): calm and easy to manage or train

ectotherms (ECK-toe-thermz): animals that control their body temperature using their environment

humidity (hyoo-MID-eh-tee): amount of moisture in the air

prey (PRAY): animal that is hunted by another animal for food

reptiles (REP-tylz): animals with backbones that reproduce by laying eggs such as snakes, turtles, and lizards

species (SPEE-sheez): one certain kind of animal

venomous (VEN-uhm-us): capable of injecting a poison through a bite or a sting

veterinarian (vet-ur-uh-NAIR-ee-un): a person trained to treat injured or sick animals

Index

Websites

www.reptilechannel.com/snakes/

www.exoticpets.about.com/cs/snakes/a/snakesaspets.htm

www.petuniversity.com/reptiles/snakes/how-to-choose/

About the Authors

David and Patricia Armentrout live near Cincinnati, Ohio, with their two sons and dog, Max. After adopting Max in 2001, it didn't take long before he won over the hearts of family, friends, and neighbors! The Armentrouts have also had other pets over the years, including cats, birds, guinea pigs, snakes, fish, turtles, frogs, and hermit crabs.